Uncommon Sense

Ammunition for
Winning the Culture War

OTHER BOOKS BY THE AUTHOR

Don't Take My Lemonade Stand:
An American Philosophy

Obama 2012 Slogans Rewritten:
Biting Political Humor on a Foundation of Truth,
Patriotism, and Wisdom

Think America Great

Uncommon Sense
Ammunition for
Winning the Culture War

Janie Johnson
Champion of Lemonade Stands

press

Minden, Nevada

RTR Press
Minden, Nevada
RTRPress@gmail.com
www.jjauthor.com

Author website: www.jjauthor.com
Author email: jjauthor@gmail.com

Printed in the United States of America

ISBN Paperback Version: 978-0-9848819-4-9
ISBN eBook Version: 978-0-9848819-5-6

Book Cover & Interior Design: Ghislain Viau

To Ray

Contents

Preface ix

Introduction: Democrat Dictionary 1

1. The Ministry of Truth 9

2. The Unmelted Pot .13

3. Vote! Dead or Alive 17

4. The Two-Income Death Trap 21

5. The Climate Apocalypse 25

6. Shut Up and Get Canceled. 29

7. It's OK to Be White 33

8. Shall Not Be Infringed 37

9. PhDs for Plumbers .41

10. Remember the Crusades 45

11. Entitled-ments 49

12. Hawk If You Do, Dove If You Don't. 53

13. The Government Spends It Better 57

14. Safe, Legal, and Frequent 61

15. Better than Bill Gates. 65
16. All Men, Created Somewhat Equal,
    Under Government 69
17. Ever Been to the Doctor? 73
18. Illiberal. 77
19. The Great Big Snowball 81
20. Free Marxist Capitalism. 85
21. The Individual, Ultimate Minority. 89
Summary 93
About the Author. 95

Preface

This book reflects the influences that tweeting has had on the United States and its capacity to communicate one on one with people around the world.

Since 2010, when I wrote my first book, *Don't Take My Lemonade Stand: An American Philosophy*, I have become dedicated to engaging in the politics of life and government. My goal in writing *Don't Take My Lemonade Stand* was to remind parents, citizens, and patriots why America is exceptional and then to teach our kids to keep it exceptional. I found out that was not enough. We must win the war of ideas—the assault on America that is happening in our schools, our media, and in our government. Thus, we must think America great.

In *Uncommon Sense: Ammunition for Winning the Culture War*, I provide an introductory sampling of twenty-one subjects with twenty-one truths to give Americans the words to win the war on American greatness. The Left often provides well-sounding talking points that simply undermine American values and worse—its lies just don't work!

In the Think America Great series of books, I will help you develop your own principles, ideas, and words to fight the insanity of the Left. The purpose of principles is to help organize thought. The purpose of organized thought is to inform actions.

My goal in writing *Don't Take My Lemonade Stand* began as an attempt to answer my then-ten-year-old son Sammy's question, "How do you know who to vote for?" During the writing process, I realized that answering Sammy was harder than it appeared, plus there were many others besides Sammy who needed educating about this matter.

In particular, I realized that parents and children from all walks of life needed to understand more about the founding of our country, the workings of our politics, and the principles on which our founders relied.

Don't Take My Lemonade Stand: An American Philosophy became a tutorial for parents, kids, and others to better understand why our country began as it did and became what it is.

During the process of promoting that book, I learned much from TV appearances with Sean Hannity, David Asman, *Fox & Friends*, and my local *Nevada NewsMakers*.

My radio interviews with Lars Larson, Monica Crowley, and others also proved enlightening. Along the way, I made countless speeches to conservative groups, and appeared on National Public Radio (NPR).

With endorsements from publishing executive Steve Forbes, diplomat John Bolton, coach Lou Holtz, news anchor David Asman, and commentator David Limbaugh, I found many loved my book and my message. But I also found that the United States and our values were under assault by Leftists everywhere!

During my Twitter experience, I offered a few mock Barack Obama slogans designed to expose the Obama presidential philosophy and contrast it with mine. After a brief time, my tweepers asked that I put these slogans into a book. My second book, *Obama 2012 Slogans Rewritten: Biting Political Humor on a Foundation of Truth, Patriotism, and Wisdom*, made history.

If you believe in an unending cycle of government dependency and wasteful spending or you are antibusiness or antimilitary—you are on the team that I oppose. If you believe in personal responsibility, limited government, free market capitalism, and a strong national defense—we are on the same team.

Please enjoy this first book—*Uncommon Sense: Ammunition for Winning the Culture War*—in my six-book Think America Great series, Common sense isn't so common!

This series of books, Think America Great (TAG), is not just one book—but a six-book series of thought-provoking conservative solutions. TAG, filled with pithy and biting wisdom, is the ammunition that everyday Americans must have to think and express America's winning conservative solutions to fight back liberals and to defend and promote the American way!

The Think America Great Series

1. Uncommon Sense: Ammunition for Winning the Culture War

2. Pray. Vote. Buy a Gun. Conservative Solutions—What Works!

3. Triggered Truths. Liberals Are Not Liberal

4. Democrat Slogans—The Names May Change but the Slogans Remain the Same

5. 2020 Campaign Ground Rules—Fake News Rules

6. The Cheese Is NOT Free—and Other Lies Government Tells You

I can be found on Twitter at @jjauthor.
My website is www.jjauthor.com.
Don't Take My Lemonade Stand: An American Philosophy,
my first book, is available online.

Happy reading!

Janie Johnson

Introduction

Democrat Dictionary

Leftists operate by manipulating feelings. They use euphemisms and misleading nomenclature when the layperson's word is too revealing of the truth. When people in Washington, DC, start creating fancy new phrases, instead of using plain English, you know they are doing something they don't want us to understand!

Democrats use these euphemisms to avoid citizen and congressional scrutiny. Worse, they think we don't know! Here are some common words the Left substitutes for reality.

1. Abortion—A medical procedure for destroying a group of cells, coincidentally shaped like a baby.

2. Affirmative action—Hiring or granting scholarships to people based on the color of their skin rather than the content of their character.

3. Affordable housing—Rent control and "the projects" (read ghettos).

4. Anti-American—Not a communist.

5. Balanced—"My way or the highway." Nothing more!

6. Balanced approach—You pay higher taxes, but democratic voters don't!

7. Bigot—Republican.

8. Bipartisan—Leftist agenda accepted without complaint.

9. Climate change—We can control global climate with higher taxes and regulation.

10. Compassion—Spending other people's money.

11. Compromise—When the Republicans cede a conflict.

12. Continuing resolution—Kick the can down the road; let our kids deal with it.

13. Controversial—Infuriatingly truthful.

14. Debt—Unlimited free money.

15. Debt ceiling—The new spending floor.

16. Demagogue—A person, especially a political leader, who gains power by arousing prejudices and passions. Synonym—Democrat.

17. Disenfranchisement—Requiring proof of identity to vote.

18. Diversity—Too many White people.

19. Economic justice—Socialist redistribution.

20. Embryonic pulsing—Unborn baby's heartbeat.

21. Entitlement—Dependencies used to control populations, redistribute wealth, and the cause of the budget deficit.

22. Environmental justice—Sacrificing prosperity, quality of life, and employment in exchange for useless money-pit environmental programs.

23. EPA—Employment prevention agency!

24. Extremists—God-fearing, red-blooded Americans who value inherent rights; anyone who owns a weapon more dangerous than a golf club.

25. Fair—Hurts the rich or helps the poor, or both.

26. Fair share—From each according to his ability, to each according to his needs. In short, Marxism.

27. Fair share—Marginal tax rates.

28. Feminism—Having a family with a man and children without premarital sex is an evil societal gender institution.

29. Fiscal restraint—Decreasing the rate at which we are accelerating the increase in national debt we are accruing, periodically, over the next eighteen decades.

30. Gender—Social constructs, pick yours like the color of your socks.

31. Government—The omnipotent guarantor of individual rights as long as you agree and obey with "The Agenda."

32. Greed—When you don't want to fork over your own money, *not* when we want to spend it for you.

33. Green New Deal—A plan to lower the global temperature by setting American infrastructure and economy on fire.

34. Gun control laws—Dissident disarmament measures.

35. Indigenous Peoples' Day—White People Bad Day.

36. Islamophobia—The irrational recognition of the dangers of radical Islam.

37. Judicial—Legislative.

38. Justice involved individual—Convicted felon.

39. Legality—Morality. If it's legal, it must be moral!

40. Limited kinetic operation—War.

41. Living constitution—The Founders were old, slave-owning, racist fools, and we know better. Let us change it. Pinky swear we will give it back.

42. Living within your means—Ditching the average Joe to starve.

43. Lying—Speaking while conservative.

44. Mainstream media (MSM)—Your daily dose of "right think."

45. Microaggressions—Anything I don't like.

46. Millionaires and billionaires—The devil.

47. Minimum wage—Under no circumstances should workers negotiate their own wages. The more people on unemployment, the better.

48. Moderate—An anchor on this glorious cruise to a progressive America.

49. Multiculturalism—The fewer White people, the better!

50. National Public Radio (NPR)—The ministry of truth.

51. Obamacare—Medicare for all; beta testing.

52. Obstructionist—Dissident.

53. Phony—Accurate.

54. Plausibility—A lie that's been parroted by enough media outlets.

55. Profit—Theft of employees' wages.

56. Progressivism (Liberalism)—This country sucks; let's change all of it.

57. Quantitative easing—Currency manipulation.

58. Racist—Republican, conservative; any non-Leftist.

59. Religious—Bigoted backward hillbilly.

60. Rent control—More homeless people, please.

61. Republican—A right-wing, gun-hoarding, hateful bigoted Nazi, or an ignorant hick who doesn't know better, or anyone in between.

62. Rich—Greedy.

63. Right—A conditional privilege granted to individuals by the government.

64. Scandal—Republican did a no-no.

65. Sequester—No, not spending. *Sequestering.*

66. Smart tax rate—Higher tax rate.

67. Social justice—Reparations.

68. Sustainability—Useless and wildly expensive environmental "renewable energy" programs to nationalize infrastructure and aggregate power.

69. Tax increase—Higher taxes on only the richest people and definitely not the middle class.

70. Tax the rich—Tax employers and job creators.

71. Taxes—Money the government doesn't trust you to spend *correctly.*

72. Tea party—Terrorists (yeah, "reporters" actually said that. On national TV).

73. Tolerance—The acceptance of all things different to our own. Except opinions, naturally.

74. Transparency—Controlled leaks.

75. Unaffordable—Anything that cannot be bought with a single, minimum-wage paycheck.

76. Undocumented immigrant—Illegal alien.

77. Unsustainable energy—Coal, natural gas, or nuclear power.

78. White nationalist/supremacist—Anyone who disagrees with us.

1

The Ministry of Truth

"The media's the most powerful entity on earth. They
have the power to make the innocent guilty and to make
the guilty innocent, and that's power. Because they
control the minds of the masses."
—Malcolm X

1. When the liberal media say, "President Donald
   Trump is not connecting with ordinary people"—how
   could they know?

2. Could we please stop calling these "reporters"
   "journalists"? They are the Democrats' palace guard!

3. Democrats have a public relation (PR) advantage:
   Media supports their ruthless lies and the rest of us
   are limited by the truth!

9

4. Democrats construct an image of reality—then the media documents it for them!

5. With Google, it seems to matter how you think, not what you did!

6. The media will never focus on the widening gap between Democrat promises and Democrat deliveries!

7. When a Democrat talks, the national media endlessly echoes!

8. Media rules for covering Democrats echo Democrats' excuses and never put any Democrat in an unflattering light!

9. I forget! Does the Democratic National Committee (DNC) give the fakers at fake news the latest talking points or does fake news give the Democrats the "news"?

10. It seems every "journalist" has become an activist with an agenda!

11. No matter what the media says, the only poll that matters is at the ballot box.

12. The national media "journalists" aren't watchdogs, but lapdogs.

13. What on earth is the defensible purpose of government radio or TV?

14. Talking points are not facts, no matter how many times they are repeated by politicians or the media!

15. When it comes to conservatives, the Left-wing media and politicians consider themselves judge, jury, and executioner!

16. A dutiful and sycophant media member must be called a "gossip columnist!"

17. One thing I learned from the media is that the people might be still evaluating the candidates—but the pundits have clearly made up their minds!

18. Is it not truly surprising that anyone was actually too foul for MSNBC?

19. We are the antidotes to much of the nonsense that comes out of the DNC and the press corps!

20. When the national media keeps repeating, "Donald Trump is not one of us," I say, thank God!

2

The Unmelted Pot

"I had always hoped that this land might become a safe
& agreeable Asylum to the virtuous & persecuted part of
mankind, to whatever nation they might belong."

—George Washington

1. Wanting a secure border has nothing to do with race.

2. If twelve to twenty-two million new immigrants
   from Mexico will help the US economy, why didn't
   they help the Mexican economy before they left?

3. So, apparently, we cannot possibly deport a million
   people, but we seem to have no problem importing a
   million and setting them up for life.

4. Democrats do not want an immigration overhaul; they want open borders and more Democrat voters! Save illegal immigration!

5. When did demanding that people come to this country legally become too much to ask?

6. Stop calling "undocumented workers" "illegal aliens"—they are "unregistered Democrats!"

7. So, if current immigrations laws are mocked and disregarded, what makes us think new ones will be respected?

8. Why do Democrats choose illegals over citizens?

9. Without border security first, immigration laws only exist on paper. There is no sovereignty.

10. What kind of danger, damage, or tragedy must occur at the US/Mexican border before Congress will secure it?

11. Imagine the Democrats' outrage if it was the Republicans importing an undeveloped country's underclass to create a Republican permanent majority?

12. If illegal immigrants began to vote Republican, our southern border would be closed within hours!

13. Illegal immigrants won't be happy until they get full amnesty and full welfare rights. Democrats won't be happy until illegals can vote!

14. "Open borders" do not exist. We either have borders or we do not!

15. The "heat" in our American melting pot is not high enough to assimilate all we are placing in it!

16. Democrats not only gave young illegals deferred deportation, they gave them work permits, free college, healthcare, welfare, housing, electronic benefit transfer (EBT) cards, and driver's licenses!

17. The true solution for resolving the illegal immigrant crisis is to replace those in Congress who will not vote to secure the border!

18. Liberals use the term "undocumented immigrant" to make it sound like no one broke the law!

19. If liberals didn't believe illegal immigrants would vote for Democrats, they'd drop them like a hot rock!

20. Democrats don't just give illegals sanctuary, they give them $ubsidized $anctuary!—with your money!

3

Vote! Dead or Alive

"I consider it completely unimportant who in the
party will vote, or how; but what is extraordinarily
important is this—who will count the votes, and how."
—Joseph Stalin

1. Only in America . . . could you need to present a
   driver's license to cash a check or to buy alcohol, but
   not to vote.

2. How big an insult is it that liberals believe millions
   of Blacks would find getting voter identification (ID)
   too onerous?

3. It is not voter suppression to require an ID; it is voter
   suppression when you allow someone illegal to vote
   or to vote two times or more.

4. It seems a bit hypocritical that unions are against voter IDs in US presidential elections but require a picture ID to vote in a union election!

5. Why are Democrats so against the US upgrading to Mexican voter ID standards?

6. Voter ID suppresses voters! It suppresses the illegal, dead, and multiple voters.

7. There is finally conclusive evidence that Osama bin Laden, Qasem Soleimani, and Muammar Gaddafi are dead. They are all registered to vote in Chicago.

8. What Democrats mean when they are promoting ease of access is—vote early and vote often!

9. By law, you must show a photo ID to buy decongestants—but not to vote.

10. What is it that liberals have against honest elections?

11. The Democrats in government still consider "voter fraud" a voting right!

12. It has to be asked: Are people who are not smart enough to get an ID Democrats, or are Democrats just not smart enough to get an ID?

13. Photo ID votes make it easy to see which political party thinks it benefits from voter fraud!

14. Is the government suppressing welfare by requiring an ID? If so, it must be unbelievably bad at it!

15. Who is it you know that is so limited in intellect or resources that they cannot get a free government ID?

16. Not having a voter ID does not stop anyone from voting. A provisional ballot is given and counted once and verified!

17. Will it take a picture ID to get into the Democratic National Convention? My guess is, it will!

18. Liberals still find it unreasonable that voters are required to be who they are—and only who they are!

19. The two sides of the voter ID issues are as follows: one wants to ensure the integrity of elections—and one does not!

20. Progressives don't fear that any American citizens will have trouble getting voter IDs; they fear that illegals will have difficulty getting them!

4

The Two-Income Death Trap

"The best social program is a job."
—**Ronald Reagan**

1. No individual can make a better economic decision than over 300 million people voting within the free market.

2. Is it possible that Democrats would rather see Americans unemployed and in need of government assistance?

3. Now that we know "freeing people from work" is a liberal objective—perhaps we better understand their many programs!

4. Democrats' economists seem to see joblessness as a "choice" to be encouraged, not a problem to be solved!

5. If you want job creation, you need innovation. And if you want innovation, you need to put capital at risk. This could not be simpler!

6. The problem in job creation is not "uncertainty"—it is the "certainty" that the Democrats will institute the wrong policies!

7. If it weren't a living wage, why would you work there?

8. Where do politicians get the numbers to decide minimum wage?

9. Minimum wage isn't meant to support a family of four.

10. Why don't the Democrats address our exceptional economy? One answer is that they do not know how!

11. When the economy is floundering, politicians first deny, then rationalize and blame—then change the subject!

12. It's more important to shrink government than to balance the budget via taxes or borrowing!

13. Keynesian economics assumes moving money from your left pocket to your right pocket can make you richer!

14. The reason we are finally seeing some positive numbers in the economy is that it took entrepreneurs and Trump to overcome Obama's policies!

15. The only "weakness" shown in the American economy has been exacerbated only by the weakness shown in the Democratic Party!

16. Democrats define "economic justice" as not having to bear the consequences of their previous bad decisions.

17. Less than 1 percent of Americans are paid minimum wage. Perhaps letting employers compete for workers isn't so bad?

18. The only job a Democrat cares about—is his or her own!

19. If Democrats cared about teenagers, minorities, and unskilled laborers, they would work to abolish minimum wage laws.

20. Employers, especially small business owners, have limited budgets for employees. Higher minimum wage means fewer jobs, period.

5

The Climate Apocalypse

"Science, however, is never conducted as a popularity contest, but instead advances through testable, reproducible, and falsifiable theories."
—Michio Kaku

1. The only "science" related to climate change is political $cience!

2. The only thing "climate change" is a threat to is science!

3. How much global-warming, alarmist hot air must we tolerate with grace?

4. The question isn't if humanmade climate change exists (not likely), it's whether anything Democrats are planning would make a difference!

5. Is it more foolish to believe in "climate change" or "climate control"?

6. When will climate change alarmists take to China and India for their overwhelming share of carbon emissions?

7. OK—tell me, is the "heat" caused by global warming, or does global warming cause the "cold"?

8. It's telling that Socialists and Communists are drawn to environmentalism.

9. What climate alarmists want most is fewer people. They each have one life to give to that plan!

10. These state and federal environmental studies often take years to complete. They are then often followed by environmental lawsuits!

11. So-called environmentalists abuse enviro studies and the Endangered Species Act to stall—hoping developers will run out of resources!

12. The word "alternative" as in alternative energy is a euphemism for "unproven" and "uneconomical" vote-buying scams!

13. Have you ever wondered why all the special clean air rules adopted in California have not cleaned up the smog and pollution?

14. If it rains—global warming. If it's dry—global warming. If it's cold—weather. If there's a storm—global warming!

15. If the world were ending in ten years, why bother saving money, voting, having kids, etc.?

16. What the warming alarmists have proved is that scientists can make a computer model say whatever they want it to.

17. The true goal of environmentalism is the elimination of capitalism and modernity!

18. For liberals, it's never been about climate change, it's been about climate change taxes!

19. Democrats will focus on their climate change hoax—their other hoaxes have been largely exposed!

20. There are few, if any, climate prophets forecasting doom who are not profiting from their prognostications!

6

Shut Up and Get Canceled

"If liberty means anything at all, it means the right to tell people what they do not want to hear."
—George Orwell

1. Let the First Amendment to the US Constitution be the speech code!

2. Who decides what constitutes "hate speech"?

3. To many liberals, most of what the US Constitution says is a "thought crime!"

4. When universities establish "free speech zones," does that imply that all other "zones" are "censored speech zones"?

5. No Democrat ever vigorously, or even limply, defends the right of free speech.

6. Everything progressives say about protecting "free speech" and "diversity" is a lie. They don't want free speech or diversity.

7. Constitutionally protected free speech appears crass to those who abhor the notion of unabashed individual freedom.

8. Democrats don't burn books in America—they now rewrite or ban them.

9. Word that best summarizes political correctness—censorship!

10. Political correctness is a Left-wing invention designed to create "victims!"

11. Brainless political correctness and hysterical overreaction are at the center of the liberal thought police!

12. Political correctness begins with identity politics and ends with an infringement on free speech!

13. Political correctness is an authoritarian endeavor to police speech in the name of protecting hurt feelings!

14. Political correctness is dangerous because it hides the truth.

15. Political correctness created the term, "undocumented worker." Are criminal killers soon to be "justice-involved individuals"?

16. The American Left today has succumbed to appeasement and political correctness—in all it does or doesn't do!

17. For too many people, the concepts of right and wrong have been replaced by the term "legal!"

18. Have you heard about the Left's demand for "trigger warnings" to alert students that uncomfortable content might be coming?

19. If you think no one should ever have to see or hear anything discordant or challenging, don't go outside.

20. Don't forget the golden rule of big tech, never make the mistake of having an opinion while conservative.

7

It's OK to Be White

"I look to a day when people will not be judged by the color of their skin, but by the content of their character."
—Martin Luther King Jr.

1. When is the time for the nation finally to put affirmative action preferences and all forms of discrimination behind us?

2. Race only matters to racists.

3. Republicans have never elected a Ku Klux Klan (KKK) majority leader!

4. Racist—Anyone who wins an argument with a Democrat.

5. Because liberals think Asians are bright and Whites are privileged, what do they think about Blacks and Hispanics?

6. The *only* way to stop discrimination on the basis of race is to stop discriminating on the basis of race.

7. It appears race hustlers want to be judged on the color of their skin—*not* on the content of their character!

8. It's racist to call others "racist"—just because they disagree with you!

9. Democrats don't support Blacks and other minorities—they use them!

10. Race-baiters make their living fanning the flames of envy and hatred!

11. The White privilege movement is a pitch against capitalism and for the welfare state!

12. Why do all the professional race hustlers congregate in the Democratic Party?

13. Race hustling is a thriving industry!

14. Where is the race hustler or grievance industry exploiter who asks to be judged by the content of his or her character?

15. Have you noticed any word is a code word for "racist"—community, neighborhood, poor, etc.? I guess when your only lens is racist!

16. Liberals keep complaining about so-called "racist dog whistles"—and they do so incessantly!

17. The people who react to the whistle always assume it's intended for somebody else!

18. Reminder—The whole point of the dog whistle metaphor is that if you can hear the whistle, you're the dog!

19. "Equal protection" does not imply "unequal protection!"

20. Affirmative action is still (and always will be) discrimination!

8

Shall Not Be Infringed

"No free man shall ever be debarred the use of arms."
—Thomas Jefferson

1. There is no "gun control debate"—the Second Amendment exists, and some fools want it not to!

2. Gun control is not about guns—it is all about control!

3. Why is it that liberals so want to disarm the population?

4. When an organization or a government entity bans guns—it in effect bans self-defense!

5. There is a gun registry in Nevada—it is called a phone book!

6. Gun control laws *cannot* stop criminals from getting guns. Laws don't stop criminals!

7. Being stripped of the ability to defend yourself makes you "safer," according to the government—liberal nonsense!

8. One thing for sure, successfully banning private gun ownership will leave nearly all the guns in the hands of criminals!

9. Reminder—As with gun control, support for immigration reform requires that which is in short supply—trust in the government!

10. Solution—It should be illegal for Democrats to own guns. Take the guns from Democrats, and you've just reduced gun crime by about 97 percent!

11. Liberals constantly decry the "power of the National Rifle Association (NRA)"—but what's really bothering them is the Second Amendment and the power of the American people!

12. The only gun rights you have in this world . . . are those you are willing to fight for!

13. This is my gun permit—the Second Amendment!

14. Liberals tell us *not* to judge *all* Muslims by the actions of a few lunatics and then judge *all* gun owners by the actions of a few loons! Liberal hypocrisy!

15. If you believe in Second Amendment rights, don't vote for a Democrat. It's that simple!

16. Picture America with no strong defense, no armed citizenry, no free markets, killing babies born alive, no healthcare, no border security, huge debts, and no energy—Democrats do!

17. #ProgressiveCommandment—Criminals don't kill people; law-abiding citizens with guns kill people!

18. #ProgressiveCommandment—Criminals need short sentences and cushy jails to rehabilitate them!

19. The US Department of Justice Operation Choke Point's goal is to stop banking services for gun companies—Democrats want your guns!

20. I'm sorry, was *Fast & Furious* an illegal gunrunning operation or just an "undocumented" gunrunning operation?

9

PhDs for Plumbers

"The philosophy of the school room in one generation
will be the philosophy of government in the next."
—Abraham Lincoln

1. Failing public schools—liberals built that!

2. Is the government even capable of improving
   education? Does the government even want to?

3. Failing unaffordable colleges—liberals built that!

4. When rich liberals send their kids to private schools,
   do they first check for "adequate" diversity?

5. Has the US Department of Education actually
   educated anyone?

6. Reminder—When we eliminate the entire Department of Education, we will not be cutting education. It does not educate anyone!

7. When liberals ruined our school system—they were on the wrong side of history!

8. How related is the deterioration of US education and the establishment of the Department of Education bureaucracy?

9. If we don't measure teacher performance, we won't manage it. If we don't manage teacher performance, it will get worse!

10. How long should we leave an issue as important as educating our youth in the hands of an incompetent government? Just askin'!

11. If the poorly educated entertainment industry can figure out how to pay the best performers the most, why can't highly educated teachers?

12. Liberals oppose school vouchers because they put the teachers' unions political contributions ahead of educating minority children!

13. What teachers and other public employees give up to protect poor performers is a reward for good performers!

14. Who would be fighting school choice if members of Congress and the government were required to send their kids to public schools?

15. Democrats continue to sacrifice the education of poor and minority children to the interests of the teachers' unions and Democrats' union dues!

16. Liberals oppose school vouchers because they want unions to have school choice, not parents!

17. Our educational system has let us down. Instead of teaching the skills to take risks and start a business, it focuses on social justice

18. Democrats' union education plan is simple: if the kids can't pass the test, either lower the standard for passing or quit giving the test!

19. Right now, student achievement is nowhere in the teacher evaluation process—so kids can fail while the teachers succeed!

20. Teachers are important, but there is never a time when taking care of teachers is more important than taking care of kids!

10

Remember the Crusades

"My concern is not whether God is on
our side; my greatest concern is to be on
God's side, for God is always right."
—Abraham Lincoln

1. The official motto of the United States is "In God
   We Trust."

2. It's freedom *of* religion, not freedom *from* religion.
   Tell a liberal!

3. When Democrats see a cross, they see intolerance
   and bigotry, and Christians will be treated as such.

4. The only celebrities who won't be mocked for
   attending church are politicians. Would they be going
   on their own?

5. Religious freedom does not end at small business. Forcing people to violate the tenets of their religion is why we left Great Britain.

6. Do liberals reject "religious values" because they don't agree with the values or they don't like the notion of religion?

7. The Democrats omitted all references to God in their platform. Is there any chance this was just an oversight?

8. Why are there no mounting protests by the so-called moderate Muslims condemning and excommunicating radical terrorists?

9. The Left denies our Judeo-Christian founding and insists that humans produce objective morality. Objective morality like abortion?

10. Liberals stepped up their war on religion—when they made it illegal to pray in school!

11. It's odd that the people who don't believe in God seem to be experts on the Bible.

12. Who are these nimrods that believe a "war on Christmas" even needs to be fought? What could they possibly hope to win?

13. Teach a man to fish and he'll eat for life. Give a man someone else's fish and he'll vote for you!

14. Muslim brotherhood—Allah is our objective; the prophet is our leader; the Quran is our law; dying in the way of Allah is our highest hope.

15. Islam is misunderstood to be violent, and Christianity is misunderstood to be peaceful, if the Left is to be believed.

16. Are there really some sensitive souls who feel coerced merely by being in the presence of public prayers? Can we get them help?

17. Why do Democrats openly hate only the Judeo-Christian God?

18. I am proud to be a bitter clinger!

19. Only secular Jews vote blue. Why?

20. Church tax exemption *will* be attacked under the guise of lesbian-gay-bisexual-transgender (LGBT) activism.

11

Entitled-ments

"Those who would give up essential Liberty,
to purchase a little temporary Safety,
deserve neither Liberty nor Safety."
—Benjamin Franklin

1. The entitlement train is rolling, the track is ending, and the liberals are calling for more speed!

2. We gave the government a Social Security Trust Fund. It took the money and spent it—not on Social Security!

3. Social Security is a Ponzi scheme and a great big lie!

4. The 1936 government pamphlet on Social Security said, "That is the most you will ever pay." Said before rates were raised!

5. The fact is you have no property right at all to your Social Security contributions! *None!*

6. Americans were sold on the belief that Social Security is like a retirement account and money placed in it is their property.

7. Congress attempts to dupe Americans when it phonies up its accounting and when it "creatively" names a new piece of legislation!

8. Government's future commitments to Social Security, Medicare, etc., do *not* appear on Uncle Sam's balance sheet.

9. Think about the term *entitlement*. If one American is entitled to something he or she didn't earn, where does Congress get the money?

10. Entitlement is a Left-wing invention that makes welfare programs sound like constitutional rights.

11. Entitlements are not debts owed—they are confiscations of other people's money, expected and demanded!

12. Entitlements are not legitimate debts owed—they are illegitimate political payoffs promised by corrupt politicians!

13. An entitlement is legal theft. Congress forces one American to pay for another American. I thought slavery was outlawed?

14. Politicians need to admit that they spent all the Social Security money and there is none left. There are only Social Security obligations, no cash!

15. Reminder—Democrats' Obamacare stole $716 billion from Medicare and gave it to Medicaid.

16. Will Congress put forward a plan to reform and save entitlements such as Medicare? Not!

17. Liberals know that Medicare and, to a lesser degree, Social Security are unsustainable, but this is not an issue for them!

18. Democrats, or rather the Socialists, want to turn Medicare from an earned benefit to a welfare program—it's just that simple! #Medicare4All

19. The Social Security Trust Fund gave its real money to the US Department of Treasury and accepted electronic IOUs in return!

20. Just as a matter of fact, all government spending (except payment on government debt) is discretionary. Change is allowed and legal.

12

Hawk If You Do, Dove If You Don't

"Of the four wars in my lifetime, none came about
because the U.S. was too strong."
—Ronald Reagan

1. Democrat doctrine aids, appeases, and abets our
   enemies; alienates, annoys, and angers our allies!

2. Why is pouring water on a terrorist's head torture,
   but vaporizing him by remote control drone humane?

3. Politicians need to realize that if they engage in war,
   that along with the bad guys, innocents will be killed.

4. Losing wars for political or politically correct reasons
   is a total misunderstanding of war and the value of
   life!

5. Only enter a war if it is both winnable and worth winning. Don't enter a war if you are not prepared to win it!

6. Iran is still dedicated to spreading terror, destroying Israel, and dominating the region!

7. Imagine defending Qasem Soleimani.

8. The liberal media would sacrifice the lives of Iranian and Hong Kong protestors to maintain negative coverage of the president.

9. Trump is dropping bombs on our enemies and cash on our allies—while Obama dropped pacifiers and blankies.

10. Appeasement only allows you to be killed—last.

11. Obama funded Iran, and Iran funds terrorism.

12. Trump has been drawing thick red lines over Obama's dotted magenta ones.

13. Iran is not moderate. Period.

14. Abandoning the Middle East will allow threats to our country to fester and grow.

15. Iran is less interested in war than the US, Iran knows it would mean complete annihilation.

16. Crushing terrorists is never a bad idea.

17. The military wants to do its job. Don't back out of lifesaving or national security operations on account of the troops. Let them do their jobs.

18. Iran and Hong Kong protestors are more patriotic than the Democrat Party that insists America is an imperial force for evil in the world.

19. Why do Democrats protect and praise terrorists and punish and criminalize patriots?

20. Don't you think the Democrats would dismantle the entire military if they could?

13

The Government Spends It Better

"For a nation to try to tax itself into prosperity is like a man standing in a bucket and trying to lift himself up by the handle."
—Winston Churchill

1. Democrats don't realize that the government doesn't make and can't spend money, unless it first takes money out of the private sector.

2. The so-called budget compromise that Democrats want is a compromise that keeps overspending and overtaxing!

3. "Rich" is a term of art used by liberals to rationalize the taking of private property fairly earned by hardworking Americans!

4. This "spending more than you make" dilemma seems to perplex most of Congress.

5. How many ways do politicians have for arguing against "living within our means"?

6. The only way to reduce the overreach of government is to reduce the size of government!

7. If excessive pay and pensions for government employees at all levels are not addressed—there is no hope to balance the budget, ever!

8. If a private company cooked the books like the government—it would be locked up in jail.

9. If government is not limited by the people, it will expand forever!

10. Any Democrat budget proposal for spending cuts means to make lives shorter, harder, and unhealthier. Democrat demagoguery already started!

11. Is there any chance that Democrats and their band of liberals really think that every piece of government spending provides an essential service?

12. There are always too many fools who believe giving bureaucrats more authority and more tax money will bring a solution!

13. Only a liberal could think spending can be cut by raising taxes!

14. If we give the government more money under any pretense, the government will waste it, use it to buy votes, and expand its own power.

15. Is there a tax of any nature that liberals do not support?

16. Why would anyone want to give an ineffective, inefficient, and corrupt organization like the US government more of his or her money?

17. If more people had to pay taxes, they would be for smaller government.

18. Because the top 10 percent of earners pay 70 percent of all federal income taxes—what is your definition of "fair share"?

19. Have you heard even one Democrat attempt to defend the fact that 44 percent of Americans pay no federal income tax? Me neither!

20. Which is more valuable: A promise from a crack addict or a promise from government?

14

Safe, Legal, and Frequent

"We have the duty to protect the life of an unborn child."
—Ronald Reagan

1. Life is precious!

2. The abortion industry does not want this question even asked. "At what point in development do fetuses deserve societal protection?"

3. If a fetus is not alive at any point in its development, why is it necessary to kill it?

4. Only a liberal could name an abortion factory, Planned Parenthood!

5. If a fetus could communicate, what would it say to the notion of pro-choice?

6. Supporting unlimited and unrestrained abortion on demand does not make anyone pro-woman!

7. On January 22, 1973, the Roe v. Wade decision legalized abortion. And subsequently has killed 66 million victims! Arguably the worst decision ever made by humans!

8. Only a liberal could equate sucking live babies' brains out with women's healthcare!

9. Apparently, the words "born alive" are not descriptive enough to inform the liberal activists that babies, not fetuses, were killed!

10. Why is it so important to liberals that people don't have to pay for their own contraceptives?

11. What on earth is the defensible purpose of the government paying for the killing of babies?

12. If you took a poll of the preborn, you would find life is more popular—even for liberals!

13. Defining deviancy often begins with reframing the issue. Abortion and sexual promiscuity are now "defined" as "reproductive rights" of women!

14. Shouldn't we call Planned Parenthood something like "Planned Non-Parenthood"?

15. Do Democrats and the media really believe that all women are in favor of abortion on demand for any reason at any time?

16. The oxymoronic liberal term for abortion is preventative healthcare!

17. The first choice of a liberal is to kill a preborn baby. If it can't be killed, the second choice is to make it dependent!

18. If the so-called "pro-choice" folks ever discovered they were wrong, how would they apologize?

19. Democrats and Planned Parenthood's commitment to abort any child, for any reason . . . is simply unshakeable.

20. If you want to maintain each person's control of his or her own body, why not give babies the same courtesy?

15

Better than Bill Gates

"The chief business of the American people is business."
—Calvin Coolidge

1. For me, the lemonade stand is a symbol of free market capitalism. And capitalism is America's engine of prosperity.

2. If you are successful, sooner or later the Left will come after you.

3. Profit promotes innovation!

4. Competition and innovation are the elements that generate improved products at lower prices. Without the profit motive, prosperity is impossible.

5. New businesses are the true engine of economic growth and job creation.

6. Business goes where it's appreciated and stays where it's well nurtured.

7. Politicians love power—so most of their legislation and regulations are designed to increase it.

8. The one thing Democrats and their regulators have successfully regulated is the growth in jobs!

9. Reminder—The greatest danger to America is our fourth branch of government: *unelected* bureaucrats ruling us out of business!

10. Career politicians are not afraid of pointless regulation or job-killing policies!

11. Reminder—Congress does not approve any new regulation. Regulations are strictly bureaucratic constructs!

12. Liberalism—High taxes, suffocating regulations, frivolous lawsuits, unchecked illegal immigration, and rabid environmentalism!

13. What politicians can't own, they want to control through excessive regulation and taxation!

14. Is there anything worse than an unelected activist chasing his or her ideology with regulations?

15. Progressivism begins with excessive regulation of markets, property, and private enterprise—but always ends with government coercion!

16. #ProgressiveCommandment—Thou shall regulate businesses we don't like out of business!

17. Progressives are primarily for big government and heavy-handed regulations. Both big government and big regulations favor large companies over small!

18. How many bureaucrats does the government employ to distort data?

19. Would you turn over control of your business to a career politician with no accomplishments?

20. Relieving regulatory pressure on business benefits everyone in the country.

16

All Men, Created Somewhat Equal, Under Government

"The society that puts equality before freedom
will end up with neither."
—Milton Friedman

1. Where did Democrats learn to live within someone else's means? Everywhere they went!

2. If you hate capitalism, you can't expect a capitalist to provide you a high-paying job with great benefits.

3. In a "perfect" liberal world, the maker of inferior products is paid the same as the maker of superior products!

4. If the US raises the minimum wage to $15 an hour, then perhaps it ought to lower welfare to the same amount!

5. There would not be so much wage inequality if liberals didn't hold so many people down!

6. Minimum wage—A liberal's way of deferring the need for education and training by subsidizing incompetence!

7. Once again, liberals want to ensure equality of outcome by bringing down the top instead of raising up the bottom.

8. Before the US needs a minimum wage hike, it needs jobs—higher wages but fewer jobs is not a solution!

9. Too many liberals think calling communism "income inequality" makes it better!"

10. Disparaging earned success in the name of "equality" is a defining element/tactic of Marxism!

11. A Democrat knows the minimum wage is intended to be a gateway job for new, unskilled workers. It was a wage never intended to support a family!

12. Apparently, the way liberals want to deal with what they call "income inequality" is to do away with high-paying jobs!

13. Bernie Sanders should be paid $15 an hour, tops! Income equality—He should make the same wage as the employees at a burger place, except they do more work!

14. Liberals seem willing to trade a massive increase in teen and low-skilled unemployment for a higher minimum wage for a few!

15. Apparently, liberals require a bit more study. How does getting rich by selling innovative products hurt the poor?

16. The liberal mandate of equality of outcomes for all requires a loss of liberty and property for many!

17. Because the top 10 percent of earners pay 70 percent of all federal income taxes—what is your definition of "fair share"?

18. The only way to ensure income equality is to keep everyone poor.

19. Attempts to equalize outcomes for the collective, by definition, include diminished liberties for individuals!

20. Has it occurred to liberals that the possibility of "income inequality" is a primary reason people immigrate to the United States?

17

Ever Been to the Doctor?

"If you believe that health care is a public good to be guaranteed by the state, then a single-payer system is the next best alternative. Unfortunately, it is financially unsustainable without rationing."
—Charles Krauthammer

1. The whole point of Obamacare was to have it fail, so Democrats could bring in single-payer government insurance!

2. Affordable care is just one of the things the Affordable Care Act (ACA) has failed to provide!

3. No matter what liberals say about Obamacare, it's still based on bribes, lies, coercions, and price controls.

4. Reminder—The Affordable Care Act doesn't make anything "affordable," provides no additional "care," and it is just an "act!"

5. If you want to know what single-payer healthcare is like, ask veterans how long they wait for surgeries.

6. If the government controls drugs and hospitals, it controls everything.

7. When liberals say Obamacare is "working," they mean government is expanding and the bureaucracy is taking control.

8. The media is ignoring the fact that Obamacare coverage eliminates most of the better doctors and hospitals!

9. The media refuses to acknowledge the obvious difference between health insurance and healthcare!

10. Somehow Democrats managed to write the ACA—without reading it!

11. Obamacare—The law liberals bribed through Congress!

12. We're from the government, and we're here to provide you healthcare—as we see fit!

13. Obamacare was presented as an act of charity for poor people but has turned out to be a tool for state power and government control!

14. One would think giving away "free" or highly subsidized healthcare coverage would have been easier!

15. Can you think of a more *ineffective* way to produce more doctors than paying them less and taxing them more?

16. Members of Congress didn't read the ACA but exempted themselves on instinct.

17. When you add the cost of state, federal, and employer healthcare bureaucracy cost to medical care—it just gets more expensive!

18. Trusting the government to "fix" Obamacare would be like trusting your plumber to do brain surgery.

19. If the government doesn't force roughly half the people to buy insurance at high prices—it can't afford to give the other half insurance for free!

20. If you like your plan, you can keep your plan is still a lie!

18

Illiberal

"The trouble with our liberal friends is not that they are ignorant, but that they know so much that isn't so!"
—Ronald Reagan

1. You can get arrested for having a lemonade stand, hunting or fishing without a license, but not for being in the country illegally—liberal justice!

2. You must get your parents' permission to go on a field trip or take an aspirin at school, but not to get an abortion—liberal justice!

3. In some states, you must show an ID to board an airplane or get a library card, but not to vote who runs the government—liberal fairness!

4. Your government believes the best way to eradicate trillions of dollars of debt is to spend trillions more—liberal economics!

5. Hard work and success are met with higher taxes, while not working is rewarded with EBT cards and free cell phones—liberal equality!

6. It is truly astonishing how many liberals do not believe in personal responsibility!

7. Thugs outside a voting site are not voter intimidation—but voter IDs are—liberal justice!

8. Your government requires all to be insured—but not all to be citizens—liberal equality!

9. It seems the right to privacy might allow abortions, but it won't keep your emails, phone calls, or health records private—liberal justice!

10. Liberals' gifts to America's youth include pot, crappy schools, abortion on demand, Plan B, infanticide, no jobs, open borders, banning guns, $22+ *trillion* debt, and shutting down lemonade stands—liberal caring!

11. Conservatives produce products and services people want to buy. Democrats redistribute, regulate, and tax what other people create and make.

12. Liberalism: Keep hope alive but never satisfied!

13. Willful ignorance seems to be the perfect characterization of liberalism.

14. Why is free market capitalism so frightening to liberals? Because there is little opportunity in it to buy votes!

15. What liberals want is to give the government more power, not over their lives, but over other people's lives!

16. Democrats redistribute wealth, because redistributing political power would come out of their pockets!

17. Democrats want their children to live as one percenters—just not yours!

18. Democrats would rather hook more Americans on government subsidies than create jobs for them!

19. Liberals help those who want to help themselves to your stuff!

20. When your family is low or out of money, do you take the liberal view that the best option is to increase your spending?

19

The Great Big Snowball

"Socialism . . . could only work in Heaven where they
don't need it, or in hell, where they already have it."
—Stephen Leacock

1. If we fail to teach our children the essential truths
   of government, politics, and liberalism's historic
   failures—they will learn them the hard way!

2. What is the difference between a democrat, a
   socialist, a communist, a liberal, and a progressive?
   The spelling!

3. When did educated people begin to believe a
   company would practically build itself, once
   government provides the roads?

4. The primary problem with big government socialism is sooner or later when you live beyond your means—you run out of means!

5. Liberals lust for redistribution of income, as long as it's not their income being redistributed!

6. Confiscation, coercion, and control are the heart and soul of liberalism and socialism.

7. The inexorable problem with the notion of a socialist utopia is that it does not and cannot exist!

8. In the vernacular of a Democrat, the concept of "fair share" still means, "You work—I spend!"

9. There would not be so much wage inequality if liberals didn't hold so many people down!

10. The only difference between parasites and liberals is that parasites understand that killing their host wouldn't be good for them.

11. Socialism—An idea so great, it has to be mandatory.

12. Socialism equals shared misery for the masses and special privileges for the politically connected.

13. Pandering is what liberals do to buy votes. Vote for liberals and they will give you other people's stuff!

14. Why is it that so many liberals seek to impose their notions of an acceptable lifestyle on the rest of us?

15. Does a Democrat really think the US would be better off if we were all poor—as long as we were "equal"?

16. If liberals are so compassionate, why do so many embrace the entrenched poverty and oppression of Cuba and Venezuela?

17. Perhaps we can say it slowly to liberals: Socialism does not work—it's a flawed philosophy and a failed idea!

18. Only a liberal would trade the unequal blessings of capitalism for the equal misery of socialism.

19. Liberalism is the politics of personal destruction! If liberals can't win—they will lie and demonize! They are paid to attack!

20. Detroit provides a future look at the whole US, if liberal spending policies are left in place.

20

Free Marxist Capitalism

"The most important single central fact
about a free market is that no exchange takes
place unless both parties benefit."
—Milton Friedman

1. If the rich didn't create all the wealth through free
   market capitalism, who would you take it from?

2. The liberals believe the present is a time for them;
   while the conservatives believe the present is a time
   for making society better for their children!

3. Accusing others of what you are actually doing was a
   favorite tactic of Russian Vladimir Lenin! Democrats
   have used it "religiously" since 1829!

4. Here's a question for anti-capitalist liberals. Without capitalism, how would you pay for infrastructure and the safety net?

5. The natural state of humans is to be free to pursue opportunity. The natural state of liberalism is to limit that freedom!

6. The worst part of capitalism for many liberals is that in this system, success often requires work!

7. How did so many liberals get rich decrying the evils of free market capitalism?

8. Liberals are OK with the concept of work—as long as someone else is doing it!

9. Liberals tax cigarettes and alcohol to reduce consumption, so why do they tax capital and job creators? Just askin'!

10. Liberals require a dumb-downed permanent welfare underclass to stay in power!

11. Social justice is a term made up by liberals to justify their taking of property from political opponents to give to their favorite donors!

12. The liberal promise is for a socialist paradise paid for with other people's money. It's an age-old scam fraught with deception!

13. Why are the Democrats so openly vitriolic and hateful? No strategy, no new ideas, failed programs, and no leadership—hate is all they've got!

14. We have to make the Left start defending socialism instead of us defending liberty today.

15. A liberal's lament is that it is, "Better to remain silent and be thought a fool than to speak and remove all doubt."

16. US ghettos are driven by liberal ideology, forged by unions, and bankrupted by self-serving Democrats catering to parasites!

17. Have you heard a Democrat explain how your neighbor making more money than you (income inequality) hurts you in any way?!

18. Democrats appear happy with the equal sharing of miseries—as long as they are equal!

19. Apparently, Democrats require a bit more study. How does getting rich by selling innovative products hurt the poor?

20. Ask yourself—Who is leading toward greater liberty or toward more government control?

21

The Individual, Ultimate Minority

"We've got to do a better job of getting across that America is freedom . . . and freedom is special . . . it needs protection."
—Ronald Reagan

1. As conservatives, we don't believe in the principles of free market capitalism, limited government, and strong defense because they *sound* good but because they *work*!

2. Conservatives are not against all government; we are against excessive, intrusive, corrupt, and ineffective government!

3. The conservative concept is simple: Help the truly poor and needy and create the opportunity for the rest to go back to work!

4. Limited government is not just a conservative slogan—it was born as an escape from tyranny and despotism. This must be taught!

5. The first principles offered by our Founding Fathers brought us prosperity and strength. They can do it again if we get back and stay on the path. Vote!

6. Reminder—Our founding principles for the past 100 years have been quietly ignored, ruthlessly thrown aside, and grossly misinterpreted!

7. When founding principles are ignored, unalienable rights are at risk!

8. The natural state of humans is to be free to pursue opportunity. The natural state of liberalism is to take that freedom!

9. Individual liberty is the most radical idea that humans have ever come up with. The natural state of humans is subjugation and tyranny.

10. Conservatism was not made out of thin air. It is rooted in freedom, compassion, and justice for all. Freedom never goes out of style!

11. Freedom is not just a utopian dream—it is a necessary ingredient in the recipe of American hope, motivation, and prosperity!

12. Profit is not just motivation to do better—it funds the safety net for our needy, our lifestyle, and the defense of our country!

13. Free market capitalism is not just an abstract economic system—it is the economic engine that provides unlimited, equal opportunity for all!

14. Capitalism is the most powerful engine for prosperity in the history of humankind. Tell a liberal!

15. If you want to see what central planning gets you, have a look at Cuba. Freedom is difficult to get and harder to keep.

16. You are either for the Constitution or you are not! You are for freedom, free markets, rule of law, and equal rights *for all*—or you are not!

17. Let our nation succeed or stumble with our values, our principles, and our way of life! Choose the American way.

18. Pray. Vote Republican and buy a gun.

19. Vote freedom—not government.

20. God bless America.

Summary

These 2020 truths are powerful. They represent the values of American patriots. These values once were universal American values that placed the future in the hands of individuals. Every American citizen was able to utilize their individual rights, their individual liberties, and their individual responsibilities to ensure a better life for all.

Leftists today no longer believe in the individual. They believe the group is superior to the individual. They mask their un-American values in a veneer of political correctness and self-aggrandizement. This ideology thrives on humans' most base and vile nature; it thrives on racism, tribalism, and arrogance.

White privilege is racism. The patriarchy is a horrendous view of history. Socialism is a fantasyland responsible for the death of tens of millions. America believes in the individuals to pursue their potential through hard work not handouts.

Donald Trump is a representation of our beliefs and us. He is not afraid to stand up to the mob and expose these ideologies for what they are. Trump is a reminder of the power a single individual is capable of—a reminder that America gives every citizen the opportunity to become a billionaire, a celebrity, or a president.

Vote for Trump and Republicans—if you believe, as I believe, in freedom and the individual. Vote for whomever makes the government smaller. Period.

Nothing matters unless we vote. Vote and take a friend. Take ten friends.

About the Author

Janie Johnson's *Uncommon Sense:*
Ammunition for Winning the Culture War
is the first in her six-book series, Think America Great!

Since the release of her first book, *Don't Take My Lemonade Stand: An American Philosophy*, in 2010, Janie has continued to be a proven conservative influence and was ranked number 105 on "Who's Influencing Election 2016?" by MIT Media Lab, Medium.com. Her tweets, thoughts, and truths make a difference!

Janie Johnson is a mom and a fierce defender of lemonade stands and free markets. She believes everyday people must and can make a difference in how they are governed. If everyday citizens do *not* stand up to big government shenanigans—who will?

Janie wrote her first book, the number-one Amazon politics bestseller, *Don't Take My Lemonade Stand*, when her then ten-year-old son asked her, "How do you know who to vote for?" Janie answered, "Whoever makes the government smaller." And only a child could ask, "Why?" It has been Janie's driving force to help remind everyone why everyday citizens must think and educate themselves about why voting matters—why conservatism with optimism and patriotism will make and keep America great.

Furthermore, Johnson has never given up nor met an obstacle she did not want to overcome. As the youngest of nine kids, she became the number-one junior tennis player in the US at age eighteen; a three-time All-American at the University of California, Los Angeles (UCLA), Pac-10 singles champion; and a top-100 tennis professional while participating in all four Grand Slam tennis tournaments. Her extensive travels around the world, as a professional tennis player, helped to inform her political philosophy.

Since leaving the professional tennis circuit, Janie has devoted herself to raising her four children and believes that everyday people can and must make a difference in our country. Her brand of common-sense conservatism focuses on children, patriotism, and optimism. She is an informed voter who cares deeply about our country and its founding principles. She represents all those who have not been particularly involved in the political process until recent events.

Janie Johnson is a graduate of UCLA with a degree in English. She is a proven success, whether playing tennis, writing books, or trending subjects on Twitter. Janie has appeared on *Fox & Friends, Fox Business, Hannity*, and over 500 radio and TV interviews. As a *Daily Caller* columnist, Janie wrote about, "Lemonade Lessons—What Average Americans Think." Her book was endorsed by Sean Hannity and made his book recommendation page.

Johnson says, "It is with great determination that we must never surrender and never apologize. Our kids and our country are depending on us." According to Twitter analytics, she influences over seven million people monthly with over 200,000 Twitter followers.

There is a meaningful battle taking place across our nation, and the unexpected following that Janie Johnson developed highlights the need for a strong voice on the right, a woman's voice, and a mom's voice. Johnson is helping lead the charge, one frustratingly true and provocative tweet at a time.

Though a registered Republican, Janie is displeased with nearly all politicians, including many Republicans. Her values are consistent with the US Constitution and the notions of our Founding Fathers. This book is written for everyday Americans by an everyday American. She firmly believes America cannot leave the education of our citizenry to our indoctrinated schools and biased media.

Follow the Author on Social Media

Website: www.jjauthor.com

Twitter: @jjauthor

Instagram: jjauthor

Facebook: Janie Johnson

Made in the USA
Middletown, DE
28 September 2020